The Twain

Poems of Earth and Ether

Rosy Cole

New Eve Publishing

Great Britain

Books by the author at New Eve Publishing

Dreams of Gold *2007 (New Edn.) 1st published 1980 Hale, London*

My Mother Bids Me *2007 (New Edn.) 1st published 1984 Hale, London*

A House Not Made With Hands *2007*

The Wolf and The Lamb, *Book One of the Berkeley Trilogy 2008*

The Mustard Seed *Children's Story/Play 2011*

Coming soon...
The Sheep and The Goats, *Book Two of the Berkeley Trilogy*

Jericho Rose, *Songs from the Wilderness* 2nd poetry collection *(Spring 2013)*

On the horizon...
The Ivy and The Violet, *Book Three of the Berkeley Trilogy*
Entertaining Angels *(Marion Grace novel)*

for Steve

WHO has not found the heaven below
Will fail of it above.
God's residence is next to mine,
His furniture is love.

Emily Dickinson

Reflections

Rhapsodies

Whimsies

Reflections

Nostalgia In Reverse

Westerlies
clouds shafted with gold
Atlantic
travellers without
frontiers

carriers
of strange prophetic
atmospheres
and scents I cannot
yet translate

Greener

This is how it is for them
the horizon shrinking
They seek a place to 'be'
but do not fit
The nesting instinct
frustrates at every turn
They sense a new horizon
their eye cannot behold
They feel for footholds
their heart no longer wants
The unreality of Now
is claiming them
Half of them is There
not Here
their treaty with the earth
outworn
Think not 'one foot in the grave'
for they are looking forward
They will view all
in multiple dimension
and encompass us anew
They're not subsumed in sorrow
The death, our grief, is ours
The grass is greener There
and we are Here.

This is natural

and how it is for them
Thank them, love them still
They are blazing a trail
They are making Way.

The Twain

On the east coast facing east -
On a west coast facing west -

It is not ocean that separates
where nothing can happen but
closure, transition in flight
or afloat, the bridging of gaps
by the famished and fugitive
from blighted crops and die-hard dogma,
with continents, long deluged,
forging a link in the chain
while billows from the opposite shore
recoil from teasing display,
arc high, gathering momentum
and, in a blue-green crescendo
that flares with diamond spume,
crash on the jagged Celtic
littoral of the British Isles
in unbridled exultation.

It is not ocean that cleaves...

But the seething earth which parts coast
from coast, a landlocked tempest.
Gold-seekers congregate to plot
exploitation of its wealth
and mark out territory, asserting

the right to proliferate
and consume with wanton pride,
inventing exclusive customs,
speaking in cabbalistic tongues
with a multiplicity
of idioms, cadences, inflections,
arranging an estrangement,
occasioning all manner of obstacles
which demand rites of passage
in a bid to conquer tribe and canyon
as they push 'from sea to shining sea'.

It is not ocean that cleaves...

I hear the echoes in your voice,
as in a seashell singing of its element,
of King Arthur and Tintagel,
of Patrick, Fingal and Columba
and, yes, oh yes, of Camelot!
You breath the mellow iambs
of my ancestral past, the snapshot phrases
and close-fashioned tones of our Mendips,
Quantocks, Exmoor and Dartmoor,
where cream tastes of the world to come
and the blossom is of cider apples
rather than the cherry tree. The wooden presses
creak and leak and flow with the memorial elixir
of the Old Country,
allowing one thousand leagues of sea
to be forded in a single heartbeat.

It is not ocean that cleaves...

On the east coast facing east -
On a west coast facing west -

Warning

(with a curtsy to Jenny Joseph)

When I am an old woman, I shall wear wine-dark velvet
in a retrospective style,
with plumed hat, tilted at a rakish angle,
and toss off a brandy in one go,
and quaff champagne because the sun is shining
or the rain won't go away,
or because a deadline has taken wing for distant climes.

I shall frequent VIP lounges as a matter of course
and rap on the door of 11, Downing Street, with the crook
of my stick and say I've no money for taxes. But you can
put the kettle on!

I shall recline on my couch with apricot truffles
and Lady Grey Tea, scanning the script of some hopeful
writer whose narrative suffers from the present imperfect
and whose pages betray dried morsels of keylime pie
which have sustained the harrowing toil of composition.

I shall hold salons where earnest young poets may air their
verses and their chagrin over royalties long imprisoned
in the fist of skinflint publishers.
I shall hear their lamentations upon editors from

the camp of the Philistines
and they shall weep upon my shoulder
at perfidious girls who giggle at sonnets
and prefer to moon over the beefcake on *Top Gear*.

Ah, what consolation those wordsmiths shall reap upon
my finely-tuned clavicle!
How I shall milk their sighs
and their misplaced ardour!
They shall learn that skin-dew is skin-deep
and divine the subtext of kid-leather wrinkles,
etched by a spirit
that has trounced ten thousand adversities.
They shall behold the slaking twinkle of an eye
fixed on shining uplands beyond the turmoil,
where eagles do not prey,
where doves pair for eternity,
where petals do not rust
and no worm excoriates the fruit,
where cancer does not consume like swarming locusts,
where there is neither health insurance
nor negative equity,
nor cynical columnists spitting tacks for effect
in hopes of sinking an overdraft.

Meanwhile, a little cerebral adventure...

Pole-trekking in the Adirondacks?
Wind-surfing off Goa?
White-water rafting in the Andes?

Dancing in the aisles at *Buddy*?
Or strutting one's stuff through *One Singular Sensation*?
And yes!
Singing the *Brindisi* from *La Traviata* with Alfie Boe...
Daring to rise from the audience and mount the stage,
unscripted, unchoreographed, in a flight of spontaneous
rapture
to discover all that was lost is now found:
a voice.

Maybe I should just test the bouncy castle
at the children's party,
or soar, forbidden, to dizzy heights
on the swings at the recreation ground,
a subject for Fragonard.

What fun it shall be!
How heartening that the heart-bypass
is not destined for a hospital theatre
but could take effect
while I am singing *Panis Angelicus*
in the Basilica at Assisi.
I shall pass from life to Life
through fleeting shadow
and leave the Dead Land...
behind.

When I am old and no longer need crutches
 and the sand in the hour-glass bears
 no more footprints.

Exile

Miss Dickinson, for punctuation,
Used dashes causing consternation,
No cryptic code her pen did stress,
Perhaps 'twas mere parenthesis.

That is to say, the truth's still dim,
The flash of light is nature's whim,
A rainbow shimmer, a dew-pearled rose,
Our glimpse of Heaven comes and goes.

The Island of Always

Forget the tally of your finer points,
Dismiss the reckoning of any you deplore,
Forget the why it went wrong
And the where it went wrong,
(Mere markers in the transition
from past imperfect to future perfect,
where the journey counts and the destination
is an evolving continuum).
Concrete or abstract,
The reasons matter not to me.
That presence close as breath,
Dilating within the heart so cogently,
Is one I recognise.
Defying definition,
It is the sum of all you are,
And are becoming,
And will be
On the Island of Always.

Where Bluebirds Fly?

They have cut down the trees
on which I hung my thoughts
for rearrangement
into coherent patterns

The branches were arteries
that turned my inspiration
into textured leaf
evergreen, sturdy holm oaks

from the Mediterranean
whispering of sunflowers
rosemary, olives and lemons
in their natural element

sportsground of squirrels
schola cantorum of rooks
the wings of collared doves
sunspread upon the boughs

On windy days they rocked
with interior knowledge
of history and compound time
frail scions now remnants of hope

They have slaughtered my trees
in the full flush of being
for fear of litigation
and rumours of frenzied gales

Mankind destroys the planet
I said to the Lord. Why must it?
Behold the new perspective, he said,
I am giving you the skies.

San Francisco's Reply

To Katie Burke who wrote a Valentine letter to her native city

My heart's forever
yours, Miss Burke, let me count the
ways you bridge that fault,

deep-riv'n below your
feet, with golden eulogy,
Narcissus himself

had no greater joy
in his reflection than mine
in your limpid eye

you exculpate my
treachery with a soulful
blink denied frail man

must I then believe
you'll not yield to the human
dance and play me false?

Ruining the Negative

At Independence Pass
perched on the scythe edge
of a predicament
did you discover
the landscape
formed a route
to Independence?

Or did you Pass?

Steady the lens
keep focused on the peaks
that way
the abyss
cannot exist
lean, and it will
become God's foothold.

In Memory

The room had a ceiling as high as the sky,
candleglow,
gilt cornices,
lucent reflection above the mantelshelf,
curved glazing
and serpentine planes to the furniture
I now know to be in the French style.
There were three or four wide beds,
set at angles,
wrinkle-sheeted,
the top covers, in disarray,
were the carnelian reds, golds, azurite blues
of the Renaissance,
like those depictions of Annunciation,
which, maybe, did not bespeak a period,
but chimed an echo of what had been,
back in the mists of Time
and the precincts of Memory.

I do not say that there were angels,
subserviant to Glory,
or a tenderly protective Madonna,
all beatific affirmation,
but there was an overarching form,
a female presence among some lesser acolytes,
inspiring peace and harmony,
ushering all to safety.

We knew we had to leave.
We were chosen emissaries,
bound on a journey without map or compass,
nor a pair of shoes between us.
We had always been close,
the Yin and Yang of the womb.
We left without goodbye, no sense of parting,
no expectation of being trapped
in the muscular maroon
of a war being waged between possession
and deliverance,
the noose pulsing about the throat,
all contact with each other severed
in singular file.
Ahead, I squinted shade
and craved and strained towards salvation,
amid hollow howls
and lungs gasping for turbid air.

Engulfed in loss, I came,
with only a dumb and deadened sense
of what and who had been.
Waves of forgetting sleep took over,
the world motioning through spindle bars.
This was how it was now,
absence hitched to hopeful advent.
I would survive the ghost land, and return.

Dog Star

(After Robert Browning)

That's my last canine pictured on the wall
looking as if he were alive. I call
that piece no blunder, now.
A Canon Powershot and sleight of hand
captured his mischief and there he stands.
Do sit awhile and be amused.
I said this camera by design, for none
saw Maximilian - Max for short - composed
and would have missed him altogether,
his rump fast disappearing in the rearguard
of a hundred miles an hour tornado,
had it not been for A1 technology
and the patience of a saintly spouse.
Perhaps Di chanced to pat a seat and say
Come, sit with me on your part of the sofa
and harken while I spin tall tales of your begetting.
His tail would wag; he loved a tale,
the rhythm lulling silky, pendent ears,
adjusting the helter-skelter of his heart
to gentler pace, his dark eyes bright
with immemorial knowledge
of spells woven by camp fires at twilight,
the day's work ably done, aroma of rabbit
run to earth, now sweating in a stockpot,

pheasant plucked of feathers, fit for hanging.
(*His*, sadly, didn't work, so why should theirs?)
Max was of noble Spanish pedigree, she'd say,
his sire and dam a coupling from the gods,
embellishing her yarn with arcane words
like 'perambulation' and 'peregrination'
that rang vague bells, and words like 'stroll'
he knew had to do with new-mown grass.
He'd listen, rapt to be the epicentre of Creation
There now, she'd croon. *Keep still. Good boy!* Click!
The flash would spark spontaneous momentum
and anguished squeals at apperception vanished,
nowhere the source of light found and rounded up.
But *Good boy* meant rusks and rawhide treats
and that magic word which, once articulated,
bound the speaker on pain of mayhem: *Walkies!*

Poppies

And are they gone to Arcady
where poppies loose no opiate dream,
nor memories of blood-inebriated soil?

Cobweb-frail, some staggered on,
mazed by sulphur stars of a millennial dawn,
torch-bearers of conquering

Was it for this, and this, and this,
they stood their ground in slimy human dissolution?
A Guernica before the fact

Was it for fool's gold richesse,
plush fields where children cannot safely roam,
and sharded streets from plunder?

Did they foresee the Crown despised
and governmental sleight of hand,
fables of Emperors' new clothes?

Vicarious and virtual the life
they died for, suffered Armageddon for,
kept fast the vault of Satan for

But they bequeathed green liberty,
imperilled now by bolting greed to halting red
Must we chance a Pyrrhic victory?

Venice Terminal

We were on a train from Padua,
racing towards the Venice lagoon,
when I spotted the child,
two years old, or thereabouts,
a halo of honey-kissed curls
and eyes of molten brown,
like molasses perpetually outpoured.
Expectant, trusting, vibrant with life,
his countenance so beautiful, he stole my breath.
His mother spoke: he gazed at her in rapture,
as if pearls of wisdom fell from her lips,
as if his joy depended on her gentling,
his mind searching the imprint
of a fable only it could measure,
the eyes grown sombre with inchoate loss
of heaven beyond a consuming gulf.

That child captured my heart
in one cataclysmic instant of *knowing,*
of being plunged into the essence of him,
while we sped from Europe's ancient
seat of learning towards deluged ways
and stones that told of mercantile pride
in affluence and influence
at this crossways of cultures,
where barques blew inshore,
freighted with silks and spices,

tea and sweetmeats, muslins,
dyes, attar of roses and
lapis lazuli blue as summer midnight,
a city where craning Gothic
confronts rich mosaics and the labyrinthine
excesses of dissembling Byzantium.

To this day, I know not if he was an apparition
conjured from some buried pining for lost youth.
Alighting at the station, I saw no trace.
But what had been rendered in high relief,
inspiring agonies of curdled joy, was forged in truth
and wreathed in the mystery of a *closer* sphere.
Suddenly, that child was everywhere!
In all the frescoes of St Anthony at Padua,
who embraced the infant and Madonna lily -
token of a fragile, stainless gift -
in the bronze statue, offering earth one hand
whilst drawing down the cherub from the skies
with the other, their fingers touching; an echo
of Michelangelo's lightning moment of Creation.
I dwelt long in the courtyard of the venerable magnolia,
ravished by eternity.

There was no sharing, no way the words would form.
Travel tickets conveyed no separate journey,
our shadowed pasts divergent and our mission matchless.
As pilgrims, it was the closest we ever got.

My unshod feet still haunt those ancient streets

in the supernal multiverse of gilt and guiltless cities.
The Vision melts the stark and leaden planes of Here.
A nun, singing like an angel, banished dissonance,
floating arpeggios that linger still in purer air.
Outside, a beggar, drunk on grappa, cringed at heel-height streetscapes,
shuffled and strained to grasp the feet of passers-by.
What is there but prayer, inspired by glimpses of
Transfiguration?

The last day, we returned to Venice, bound for home.
His nagging pain, dismissed by medics, was graven in
fatigue.
Metal wings clove terrestrial darkness, new dawns
forgotten.
We have been blessed and fortified for this, I thought.
A week later, they handed him over to palliative care.
There was nothing to be done.
The dream of far-flung shores and bold discovery, just that.
By summer, he was gone.

White Shirt

With white shirts, he said
the pain is that stains proclaim
your ineptitude
in a competitive world
blighting self-esteem

Dripped cappuccino
spinach, lentil soup, red wine
are markers of taste
and habitude and hunger
A neat paradox

But the choice is smart
even after Labor Day
I said. Obama's
an iconic trendsetter
It comes from the top

They suit you, I said
You wear pristine honesty
on your sleeve, or front
You strive against the tide for
the immaculate

That's Hope triumphant
You're no whited sepulchre
sporting a dark shirt

You wish the Cloths of Heaven
and Resurrection

Behold, I Stand And Knock

(Inspired by Christ, the Light of the World painting by William Holman Hunt.)

Behold, I stand at the door and knock,
It's barred and bolted fast,
The windows, blind, outface the light,
Day's dark from first to last,
The threshold bears no 'welcome' mat
For he who shrinks inside
Renounces love and laughter
And chooses there to hide.

I know his brow's impaled on thorns,
His limbs crack from the rack,
His pain's the selfsame one as mine,
He's neither purse nor pack
But seeks alone to pay the price
For others' lack of love,
I did it for him long ago
To leave him free to move.

He claims he's Doubting Thomas,
Wants to see my wounded flesh,
Can he not feel it in his own?
Does his heart with mine not mesh?
My will is for his happiness,

His peace, but where it fails
Is in the purblind turning from
The imprint of the nails.

He takes it all upon himself
To put the world to right,
For him, there's no yoke easy,
No burden that is light,
He tows the past, a willing ox,
And shuns his liberty,
But mortal love's not full enough
To brave the green hill's tree.

One day, he'll come to know me
As his own bone and blood,
The shadow and the substance
Of all he would and could,
I tread his path, I know his frame,
There's nothing I condemn,
A glance into my eyes would show
Reflections of his own.

I want to set his soul aflame,
Teach him to sing my song,
To fling his cripples crutches
In the fire where they belong,
I seek to break the cynic's heart,
Turn water into wine,
Take his mistakes and mend them
And make his troubles mine.

But now he cowers within the pale
Of loneliness and fear,
The world is cold and hostile,
The enemy is near,
I'm ranked with all the others
who put him in the dock,
But I'd transform his night to day,
Behold, I stand and knock.

Entanglement

Some have the knack of it,
how to steal under the radar
and shoot a synapse
between two continents,
theirs and yours,
with magnetic intelligence
that knows neither logic
nor calculation,
nor pheromone,
nor the twinkling eye,
nor yet the influence
of wheeling constellations
and a sovereign sun
pivoting the light,
revealing by degrees
and fickle moods
of the barometer
the profile of a character.
Some need no context.
They are an elemental Gift.

Neptune's children,
flying the governance of Mars,
know nothing of ramparts.
Their sublunary self
is their shadow.

I Know Why the Caged Bird Doesn't Sing

I know why the caged bird doesn't sing
And why God-given feather falls in spring
The ruthless month bespeaks regeneration
And flight from climes that temper inspiration
To climes where climbs the stallion sun
Envoy of death-blows dealt and done
Vaulting the hurdle of the season
Whilst overruling rhyme and reason
Reckless florescence bursts its stays
And bears blind seed of future days
Rain-sown in heat and glorious folly
Oblivious of winter's volley
For Sibylline November wreathes
The Hope that free midsummer breathes
It mulches cankered autumn sepal
Reveals the worm within the apple.

In gilded prison with wings pent
The linnet mourns his element
Preserved from naked thorn and frost
Whilst honeyed halcyon days are lost
Spent life can yield – the seasons show it
But the caged bird can never know it.

Single Character

A letter
can change
the meaning
no, not that kind
of letter
letterheaded,
stamped,
addressed,
faxed,
or emailed;
a single
letter,
from a
single
 I
to a single
You,
no, not that kind
of *You,*
U,

For instance,
to make
'collusion'
out of
'collision',

one must
substitute
U for *I*,
though, here,
You for *I*
is good, too;
and when
or
is stretched to
our,
that's neat.
Sometimes,
 a tell-tale
U
can span continents

Saying Goodbye

There are no endings, he said,
only new beginnings.
You can leave your past
in the confessional
and start from scratch,
tabula rasa every week,
admittance to High Table,
though you may deserve to be
below the salt. Or wandering
in the dark outside,
aimless, footsore and lost.
You can sup with the best
of them. It's easy, he said,
once you sign up to Belief.
The burden of consequence
is removed from your shoulders.
The Good Guy left an open
tab behind the bar.
We can party till the sun
discloses rapture at Dawn.
Breathtaking Revelation;
the lark suspended in song,
the dove composing his wings
at our feet, silver-leaved
olive twigs straddling his beak,
while the tide creams ashore
and our ear grows attuned to

celestial harmonies
shimmering through glassy air.
It's all free, he said,
once you beard the deluge,
wade in over your head,
and emerge cleansed.

He lay on his air-filled mattress,
shrunken to the bone,
(echoes of the party faded
and the sun refusing to show)
host to an alien species
that gloated in its power
to replicate itself at speed,
a miracle of entropy,
robbing him of form and function.
I never did finish weeding
the rosebeds, he said. Perhaps
I'll feel better next week.
You will, I said. And meant it.
Can't help wondering about
purgatory, he said. It's been
playing on my mind.
What's it like, do you think?
This, I said. It's like this.
Mercifully, it's nearly done.
For the first time ever, he turned
no blind eye, did not ransack
dreams of cruising distant
islands, but fixed mine for

a daunted second, registering
a shaft of accusation
at betrayal.
I was on the other side!
He never could bear endings
and slipped away through veils
of changed perception without
a murmur of
Goodbye...

Had we come so far to tell a lie?
It haunts me still
and maybe always will.

Vermeer's Muse

I am passing through
a sequence of spun still frames
shedding, showering
rhythmically recycled
ephemeral dust

This too solid flesh
belongs to time's illusion
I am a whisper
in your head, a quickening
of the soul's marrow

I am mere cipher
reflection of perception
I, a backward glance
down the halls of memory
or glimpse of future past

Yet am I present
in the consummate design
unpolished carbon
scintillating in the beam
of a loving eye

I am passing through
one, two, three, four dimensions
God exquisitely

aligns the daguerreotype
eternal lustre

Fall Guy

On November 5

The night sky sparkles with fake stars
dying at the peak of purest brilliance
and sizzling, whining blasts of sound
celebrate broken bondage to the past.
St Peter is defied to tread our soil
in Roman sandals.
The joy of it!
To claim one's heritage
through tinsel Absolution!
To scorn the screeching shackles
that once bound chafing earth
to Heaven; the psyche purged
of Purgatory and Penance,
and Hell itself,
reminders banished in an
iconoclastic frenzy stampeding
through the land,
demolishing its sacred pillars,
its effigies of Christ,
painting out its Virgins, saints and martyrs,
its presiding angels, and itself into a corner,
making church walls pale into insignificance
and imitate the 'whited sepulchres' of gospel fame.
After The Fall, the Fall, in the Fall.

Tonight a Bonfire of the subtler Vanities
takes place. Some of our forefathers
recognised the heresy of Relativism
which makes each his own god,
subscribing to self-made rules
in a solipsist cosmos doing battle
for mortal freedom
and inner peace
and blessed purpose,
jostling for a place in Paradise
secured with credit card and inflated renown,
or a Government with sublime benevolence.
The Church made Flesh was never perfect,
its faith undercut by human reasoning
and marauding logic; its power appropriated
by a hierarchy keen to rule the world itself
in God's name, whilst it divined
no curse in its flight of hubris,
nor that the founding tenets
had not moved an inch to left or right.
And still the wounded longing
for Restoration and scars repaired,
the pilgrim's staff abandoned
and the Cartographer dismissed.

At dusk, a Fall Guy mounts dead wood
to blaze in a convivial holocaust,
a parody of the soul's refining fire
and the fate of martyrs at the stake.

When Love Burned Through The Draperies

When love burned through the draperies
My soul did start, ill-clad
I sat before the mirror
And found nought to make me glad
Still steeped in sleep and darkness
And hibernation's maw
I had no mind for visitors
When love rapped on the door.

A wreath of advent candles
I'd counted one to five
then shrank at celebration
with no worthy gift to give
The silence gathered round me
like snow upon a tomb
I nursed a withered heart from grief
weaving yarns upon my loom.

The threads were bright as silver
outlining every cloud
The reds were warm as berries
and told not of blood that flowed
The blues belonged to April
The greens were plucked from May
while autumn's incandescence
was the richest irony.

I had no truck with winter
my windows fastened tight
my doors were lagged with sackcloth
my cinders warmed the night
The adamantine rime did glint
upon the stricken willow
Rain and gales vented spleen
but I clung to my pillow.

So little did I understand
cocooned within the womb
that heaven declared a rebirth
and all my senses dumb
would wake like Lazarus and dance
and all my mourning maim
when love seared through the draperies
and set the door aflame!

Mirror

Charades, you said of the clouds
read them as tea-leaves
they will interpret your dreams
and soulful wishes
truer than faltering hope

Nebulous they may appear
playful, elusive
but their substance is constant
as fine-tempered steel
They are guide and guardian

They shield when the light is fierce
chiaroscuro
is their genius; falls of
tears and noontide smiles
are vapour of living forms

A Different Way

The Virgin Speaks

We had to go a different way –
I suppose it was to be expected –
Taking the path that snakes down into Egypt
And the rufous sands of our kindred
Country, shuffling the stones out of place,
The vegetation, itself acicular,
Resembling our abraded mood,
Fraught and fugitive.

Forewarned by a compelling dream,
We speedily forsook our homeland
And the shabby stable enshrined by Grace
Wherein the Spirit of our True Abode
Consumed us in its shimmering vision
And we did indeed *possess*
That Kingdom promised to our
Forefather, Abraham.

How soon the world's rapacious jaws
Were poised to trap the infant Hope of Israel.
Herod trod the warpath, his blood up, lest he be called
To forfeit power. Rather slay the nation's
Innocents, be sure the threat has died
The death, feasting can resume

And the illusion that he alone
Invents salvation.

No resting-place, no refuge then,
The night air gnawed the cheek-skin
Yet the firmament above hosted the selfsame stars,
Their aspects changing subtly,
That guided men of wisdom,
Rulers of the East, and honest shepherds
From a cold and rocky altitude
And garnered them.

Oh Abraham, revered patriarch!
Spearhead of our toilsome path,
God pledged a race as populous as gems of heaven,
And you believed, but could not trust the manner
Of its coming. You, childless and disdained,
Took matters into your own hands,
Abetted by Sarah, true daughter of Eve,
And begot elsewhere

A bastard line, the Ishmaelites,
Born of your housemaid, Hagar, who scorned
Her mistress' shrivelled womb and barren years,
Earned persecution for her spite and fled
Into the wilderness. It was those ancient footprints
We, the Holy Family, retraced, adjusting
Cosmic balance that quarter might be
Given to exiles.

Time's passed, is passing, will pass,
The sum of it , the essence, still distilling
I am caught up in paradise no mortal mind
Can bear the telling of. All *lives*, breathes peace
Unclench your fist for Eucharistic Bread,
Earnest of that age-old pact, and you will
Richly gain a foretaste of this Land,
Bending to prayer.

The strife on earth does not abate
And conflict scars the centuries for Jew
And Arab cousins. No ploughshare, no pruning-hook
Their arms foretell. Ire explodes and gushing blood
The soil stains. Sheol needs no further depths
When they distrust God's will, an inalienable
Commonwealth, plum rich, and blindly shun
His Different Way.

A Rock and A Hard Place

There is only God
and mammon
the choice, fear or love

The dilemma's clear
as crystal
universal truth

Spiral upwards or
spiral down
the latter's easy

Let's procrastinate
dump options
take it all on board

Nothing's black and white
if we've learned
anything, it's that

Monochrome exacts
penalties
drawing lines is hard

Safer to stumble
around in
dove mists of default

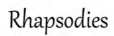

Rhapsodies

Between The Rainbow And The Dove

On the Feast of the Transfiguration

We followed him through the foothills of Tabor
leaving the world's clamour behind
sounds muzzled by distance and heat-haze
and the remoteness
of another sphere
the sardonic scree irking our toes
but we climbed
dauntless as mountain goats
glad of the umbrous oaks and green-beaded olives
offering a truce between Heaven and Earth.

The hillsides glowed pink with rock-rose
the yesterday, today and tomorrow plant
which spends its petals prodigally
and births new buds
with glad abandon
Our feet clove galaxies of groundsel
the glory of Joppa
like miniature suns
while bees gleaned pollen from the Nazareth iris
and the white-bosomed dove marked our progress.

All about us, the hum of millennia
a tranquillity not to be found on rooftops

It seemed to embody history, but renounce it
the clanging cymbal of Rome
the clumsy fist of Herod
dispersed to dust and dereliction
and we catchers of fish
and fishers of men
on the dynamic threshold of a new order
might expect the desert to blossom as the rose.

I wished Andrew could have been with us
Our meagre catches lately weighed him down
He was cumbered with holes in the network
and daily bread wasted
not cast upon water
The family needs sustenance, he said
Caring for others
he understands that
We left him working fingers to the bone
fully equipped for when the tilapia rose.

Once, I took a coin from a fish's mouth
Whose head does it bear? The Lord asked
Why, the Emperor's, I said. Whose else?
Then yield him in kind
and accord God the rest
You'll have treasure in Heaven
The memory smote
linked to my brother
for, that day, he chose the way of mammon
and marred faith's vision.

We lingered to drink at a waterspout
Rock overshadowed us, like shelter
The scene fell under the Lord's surveying eye
his brow brooding
his heart leaden
Down there, he said, in a cloudburst
did Barak defeat Sisera
the Canaanite chariots
grounded and confounded by God's hand
Deborah's faith molten in song.

Time's steed was bridled for one split second
The hoarse roar of the embattled
assailed us, the collision of star-crossed steel
weapons washed in blood
terror-stricken mounts
bone architecture smashed, vitals pierced
God's hand sustaining
but not ordaining
Psalms of promise trampled in conceit
the price of shadows lent form.

We saw his harrowing, the sun half-hid,
as if he gathered what was to come
The dove crooned its lullaby lament
The fountain quivered
A rainbow shivered
and rendered him in gold inenarrable
discrete and in relief

Oh, such relief
as transported us to where no pain was!
Glimpse of our uncharted journey's end.

First Day

New brooms and turning tides
herald the Arian brides
Ram eschews paternity
Ewe gloats in maternity
The fields are flocked with cumulus
Virescent life mocks winter's tumulus
Lambs frisk on boughs torn down by gales
Joy inspires their catkin tails
Arcadian memory revives
and the migrating swallow dives
and cleaves the newly-sunbathed air,
steam-shimmers sodden moss up there
in eaves where martins make their home
from twigs and neatly-rendered loam
In swelling lakes, the char fish rise
teased by the anglers' cunning flies
and bullion ripples spread to shore
where nutshell boats are left to moor
The cormorant is poised for kill
ready to strike below the gill
The fern unfurls primeval fronds
while frog-spawn hides in lily-ponds
In silent reeds swan cygnets hatch
March hares essay a boxing match
in thickets tangled with trefoil
and violets, and pennyroyal
thrusts up its minty lances proud

on commons where fresh nettles crowd
burdock and recoined dandelion
budding loosestrife and campion
The gorse's tines begin to gild
and daisies star the browsing field
By stealth, the spectral bluebells glow
in woods where creeps the dew-eyed doe
Larks suspend themselves in song
above their heather-feathered young
And collared doves perch on the gate
while all creation seeks its mate
Nature is bent on new beginning
and death has not a chance of winning

For us, the Ides of March give way
to shamrock and St Patrick's Day
To Riverdance and red saltire
and legends told by peaty fire
And rippling harps and Celtic airs
stir ancient pulse and haunt the ears
And lo! The equinox is past
and spring is ushered in at last!

Our Lady contemplates her dearth
When Gabriel descends to earth
and tells of Everlasting Birth.

A sword will pierce her heart, she knows
Within her womb an infant grows
Who'll light the way and conquer foes

The Lily and the Cross are bound
The Thorn springs blossom on the Crowned
And Time turns round without a sound

And as for me, an April child,
the bluebell month is never mild
The birthday joy and sorrow bind
to shadow perfect peace of mind
The day my life was to begin,
I parted from my stillborn twin.

Hero

On Palm Sunday

The air is fanned with feather fronds
The ground is strewn with boughs
A makeshift carpet tells the way
And straightened path avows

I go surefooted as a goat
Upon the mountain heights
My precious cargo is a Lamb
Prepared for sacrifice

I know I am a stubborn beast
A lissom colt untrained
My pilgrim rides as we are one
My back is never strained

The sun beats down, my tongue is parched
A mirage slakes the eye
To go the second mile with Him
The mirage does not lie

The cry of jubilation swells
The crowds love a parade
Their conquering hero comes to free

Those mighty Rome enslaved

And is this whom my forebears shared
Their stable crude and stark
When heav'n bowed down to gather earth
And wheat-gold light quelled dark?

He goes towards his destiny
Where brutal malice stings
And history will ever tell
I bore the King of kings!

Prodigal

The day spills
the contents of its
compartments

and seeks a
restraining order
that's not spring

Perhaps not
what God intends in
Holy Week

Release

The oak tree
symbol of England
vies with beech

light drenching
lime-green canopies
of birthed leaves

fan vaulting
excites fancies of
cathedrals

this April's
Resurrection sun
harps descants

mean winter's
starving frost entombs
no longer

strained bonds snap
and glorious Life
is proven

the world breaks
into harmony
He's Risen!

Who Walks With Me?

Who walks with me along my ways
Of bruisèd reeds and wavering flax
Amid the feather rye that sways
And hides the parched earth's cracks?

Who walks with me past guelder rose
And brambles scrambling to conceal
The hazel boughs and blackthorn sloes
The bindweed's healing peal?

Who strolls among the buttercups
A galaxy of saffron gold
A clover bee its nectar sups
In amethystine folds?

Who walks with me on woodland paths
Beneath translucent arches green
Where Sisley's bluebells fragrance wafts
And hints at lands unseen?

Whose tracks imprint the stony miles
Pounded by boot and flinty shoe
Whose hand spans barbed and broken stiles
And points to pastures new?

Who whispers that all will be well
When linked we promenade the shore
On blotting sand and broken shell
I would know who you are.

In Good Coin

Now shrinks darkest day
in shadow
in defeat eclipsed

Zenith has no truck
with nadir
For one void second

the hemisphere is
suspended
in eternity

in league with heaven
death cancelled
genesis regnant

December solstice
craves summer
conjures fire and light

A dim reflection
straining hope
for wild renascence

It cannot exist
by itself
without reference

to the prolific
which burgeons
glows with energy

Spin the coin and it
always falls
on the shining side!

Vacation

Some like iridescent peaks
as daylight fades through fondant veils
of rose and peach
and alphorns and laryngeal arpeggios
echo in the feudal valleys
and summon sprites from peepholes
to the land of fairytales.
Here, scarlet toadstools spring,
edelweiss, blue gentian and alpen-rose,
and cowbells clank their altitude
in misty, leather-bonded notes,
Habsburgs, long forgotten, and life itself
illuminated script,
Zwingli, a faded legend,
and Rome's hard-pinching shoes.

And some seek empty, bone-bleached skies,
inlets where Mother Earth nurtures
swan-chicks and grebes,
and stately reeds and velour rush
stand sentinel about the shell-cooped
brood corralled beneath a snowy pen,
rapt in harmony with nature.
The grebe pilots her zebraed sprigs;
their lesser vectors print the nursery tide,
estuary-bound, where billows buffet,
and rasped hulks of fishing boats

careen upon the pebbled shore
beneath tufted dunes, sea-kale and holly,
and those beribboned rockpools
in which hermit crabs reside.

But many seek exotic climes,
where zephyrs kiss sun-burnished skin
and agitation fades.
All that *was* is gone, a broken, fretful dream.
And why was it, and where was it?
Where did it go, usurper of content?
For this is surely Paradise, as meant.
Light-cut aquamarine floats in,
promise glints in silken sand,
palms whisper healing incantations.
All is divine fruition, slaked thirst, bounty:
elemental memory plumbs deep,
when lung and limb came up for air
and strove through fecund loam
to cognitive reflection.

Oh, Do Not Give Me Sunrise

Oh, do not give me sunrise
with day unbirthed
its head rising between poles in
conflict
dawning of dismissal
from a brighter sphere
shrunk to oblivion
in the womb of night
the sea's bloodbath gilded with
promise

And do not give me sunrise
on teasing cusp
of an epiphany that cannot wax
amidst a galaxy
of solipsist worlds
whose ebbing heartbeats
crave unpolluted air
and epic rest and consummation

Oh, do not give me sunrise
apprehensions
of things that might and mustn't
come to grief
tales of fair Avalon
unreached, and longings
withered to a fault

for want of nurture
in fallow field at season's sowing

Pray, do not give me sunrise
with ravelled skeins
of untold histories and mysteries
designs untapestried
to be single-stitched
by fumbling fingers
in taut laboured hours
eyeless in Gaza and as a slave

But rather grant me sundown's
laurels
blood fire-consumed!
an Indian Summer of the senses
spent flesh telling, spirit
hailing the far shore
shuffling loose the coil
while mystic music
in surround sound shuns costly cadence

New Threshold

evening sky suspends
the august moon, a bubble
of polished nacre
igneous sun capsizes
in spreading tangled
flight of seraph's silken wings

night air presages
the biting breath of ground frost
berries bloat with juice
flushed dog-rose whispers vespers
briny wind floats chaff
from sleek and spiky stubble

deer parade antlers
now the velvet glove is off
rutting and courting
prelude new generations
bone tangles branched bone
with primal ululation

capillaries fail
tendrils strain their sluggish shoots
cupped acorns harden
browsed by streaking silver form
best culled ripe and tanned
beech mast shells the forest floor

gull pins salty eye
on aerial dance of swifts
and swallows whose mind
homes on tropic Africa
cradle of mankind
Albion his own again

day and night make truce
bronze the light and celadon
rain-stippled winds blow
defiant autumn blazes
anaesthetic June
had not this tingling vibrance!

Equinox

Virgo greets Libra,
pinion of the solstices
holding in tension
summer light and winter dark
a truce between them

tides mock ebbing sap
harvest moon a memory
echoes of dancing
in barns crammed with tarnished stalks
severed from quick grain

birds seek the high wires
melodies upon a stave
designed to carry
messages of other sorts
of hope purged of pain

the season's foils come
spinning down in gales a-whirl
deep-tinctured hues of
the Renaissance period
an eloquent twist

mortal senses pique
at summer's reckless reprise
while subtle odours

of decay spike mists filming
a pumpkin-gold sun

Earth already boasts
proliferant mysteries
flagging the far side
of the arc with lustrous jade
blades of next year's wheat

Heraldry

On the Feast of St Michael and All Angels, September 29

Is this how it should have been?
Day's conflagration bids farewell,
secedes to night's increase,
above the shadowed downs and hills
an ash of silhouetted leaves
and purple isles adrift in sheen-still seas

Fawns sporting soft suede pelts
consort in dappled shade
and flinch at crackling sound,
leap ditch and nettle-bed,
and teazles stand their ground
where angels pass among the thistledown

The seedheads' broken spheres,
like melting moons, float forms
upon the breath of destiny,
green bloom of wheat on purl-ribbed fields,
a silent, living testimony
of grace through winter's whining threnody

Unsheathe your sword, Crusader!
Halt rampaging gods of mammon
that rape the earth and starve the poor,

cohorts of a deviant Demon
whose scorched earth feeds no widened maw,
whose glamorous light beguiles Hell's door!

Lady Poverty

On the Feast of St Francis of Assisi, October 4

Lady Poverty, I wed thee,
Stripped of raiment woven gold,
Seeing that 'twas Love that bled thee,
so my soul should not be sold.

I lay down my velvet mantle,
Shoes of hide from Tuscan Plain,
Coins of silver by the handful,
A rod of iron, pursuit of gain.

Oystered silk, embroidered tabard,
Fair exchange for daily bread,
Feeds the famished, shames the niggard,
Recognises leper's tread.

I renounce the life that shone bright
In revelling of troubadours,
Dancing in the streets past midnight,
Masking Satan's deadliest hours.

Sir Brother Sun and Sister Moon,
Read repentance in my alms,
Squandered riches garner no boon,
Sackcloth habit hath no charms.

Brothers Wind and Air, I call thee,
Sister Water, Brother Fire,
No more shall my deeds appal thee,
Heaven my faint heart will inspire.

Mother Earth who well sustains us
With fruits and herbs and radiant flowers,
Banished be the greed that maims us
And destroys the peace God showers.

Sister Death, your toils benignant
Shall release us, not alarm,
To that Country, our assignment,
Where no fiendish spirit harms.

So bear witness to my marriage,
Lord of Heaven and earth and sky,
Birds and beasts assist my courage
We shall gain Eternity!

Swan Song

On the Feast of St Cecilia, November 22.

The days are sweet with lavender,
rosemary, hibiscus and lilies,
bees suck petal-satin throats,
thrum a hum of multiverse,
melting veils, imparting honey
to chaste Cecilia's song.
Emollient the olive groves and tart the lemon.
The vines are drenched in peridot
and geckoes dart among the leaves.
Night crickets throb their notes in sward
and moonstruck pines whisper of the sea,
a soothing, plangent litany.

Footfalls upon the tessarae:
wafted air strums kithara strings,
proposing chords celestial
and plucking nerves.
He is come out of the Alban Hills,
a patrician youth whose profile scythes,
keen and lean; relief of chiselled limbs,

taut with harnessed power.
A pagan son whose object deities
beguile, confuse and disappoint.
He is a god himself, Valerian,
rooted in rock like the plant.

Now the string bends to the arrow
and nature reins her mettled team.
How can fidelity to Christ,
the Son of Man, be reconciled
with obedience to parents
and to unreplenished earth?
Dashed promises, like amphorae
shattered upon ferrous earth,
let spill the Water and the Wine
of heavenly banquets.
This marriage of uneven yoke
must stake or break Cecilia!

The song dies in her breast.
What manner of having and not having
is the truth of it? But vows!
The dilemma has her seraph mute.
Speak, Guardian! she cries,
bending the knee in heart-wrung prayer.
Fear not, the Angel says, *be wedlocked,*
explain the plight, bid thy spouse
meet me in the Appian Way,

trust, and he shall change his tune,
in honour bound and shared virginity
to bear the Cross of Christ in melody.

Noble Valerian, yet a heathen,
so loves his wife, he dreams her dream
of flesh dilute in ecstacy of being,
no ebbing passion, no turgid clay,
and strikes out on the flinted road
only to meet the Blessed Pope himself.
Urban's eloquence spurs bold revision,
points out a bearing strange but close at hand.
Polyphony enchants Valerian's return,
the bridal bower, thronged with lark and thrush,
rings with blended harmonies
of mortal and immortal themes.

A chaplet of roses, barbed with Thorns,
adorns Valerian's brow. The Angel smiles.
Cecilia's braid of lilies honours
an ever-bountiful Madonna,
but no sword has pierced her soul as yet.
The golden couple tread the Narrow Way,
and strive and sow in grief and gladness
under a jealous Emperor's rule,
their simple faith and sunlit vista obscure,
a threat to pride and overweening power.
Be sure that buckling reason will hold sway

and rob the life that yields eternity.

They fell the bridegroom where he stands,
neither do his convert kin escape.
Three times the axe is laid on sweet Cecilia's neck
and three times is repelled.
Her songs of praise they cannot sever,
even as God's Mercy claims her.
So Love released induces this world's tears,
till every sound becomes the Music of the Spheres.

A Pilgrim's Prayer

That hearth and home may
Hint of heaven and
Autumn's consummation
Nourish the latent seed of Spring,
Kindling a vision of that
Sweeter country where
Germination sinks deeper root and
Indicates a perennial harvest our
Vagrant span is blind to, dead to,
Imparting
Notions of perpetual
Growth in God.

Long Expected

Between the Horizon and the Foreground
lies the focus of perspective.

Between the Idea and the Vision
lies undaunted faith and a steady eye.

Between the lamp and the flame
lies the replenished oil.

Between the Servant and the Master
lies humility and undying trust.

Between the Crisis and Deliverance
lies providence and disguised blessing.

Between the Winter and the Spring
lies the Epiphany.

Between Paradise Lost and New Jerusalem
lies perpetual Renewal.

Between the Messenger and the Nativity
lies incarnation within a human frame.

Between the Father and the Son
lies an earthly Mother's love.

Between the Desire and the Arrival
lies the fusion of the spheres.

If Winter Comes

April is the cruellest month, the poet says.
Green shoots and blossoms make
a mockery of winter's torpid incubation,
the sky's sheen like old ceramic
crazed with sapless boughs,
the ponds stagnant with rotting vegetation
and hedgerows, once decked with flowers
and spangled fruit, become
naked tangled thorns,
defensive as razor-wire.

Summer's dream is banished
by the first frost, sharp as ammonia,
its sense, its scent, its sentience
suppressed in resting earth.
We don weatherproofs and scarves and rugged footwear
against gale and snow and driving rain.
We close our doors and light our fires.

Hibernation seeps into the marrow,
blunting the senses to loss of balm
and cordial breezes, chromatic tones
that electrify the filaments of nerve and fibre
and promise Paradise.
Benumbed, our grief is tamed. We shut out
the nocturne of the winter solstice
and devise our own illumination,
scorning the antipodean canicule.
We make merry with old songs,
embellishing the murk with gold and glitter,
and heart-reviving greens and reds
mnemonic of crataegus, said to heal
that restive organ of its strains and pains.

What we need is a Death to conquer death,
a Life whose Grace and Incorruptibility
can harness all the vital forces of Creation
to taste the Lethe and live to bridge its banks
Eternally.
What majesty on earth can *that* accomplish?
What man-at-arms? What president? What ruler?
Brute myth where human and divine converge!

But hush! A rumour whispers through the darkness

and there are angels carolling a new theme
when the wavelength is attuned.
A blinding star fixes the conjunction
of heaven and earth and turns
Time back to front.
No clockwork mechanism now.
A baby in a makeshift cradle
(or is it an unconstraining grave?)
signals a true Renaissance
that stirs the ailing cosmos,
pulls sap towards the ether
and consigns the cruellest month
to history's past imperfect.

Whimsies

Sanctuary (Divine Comedy)

"My mind's sunk so low, Claudia, because of you, wrecked itself on your account so bad already, that I couldn't like you if you were the best of women, or stop loving you, no matter what you do." Catullus.

Poor Claudia! 'Twas ever thus!
Since Adam's frame was formed of dust,
And Eve was taken from his rib,
She was his offspring, born to quib.
Without her he had been forlorn,
Roamed in the Garden all alone.
He sensed he had no complement
When plucking fruit all passion spent,
No mirror for his lofty soul,
No praise when he had reached his goal,
No one to cheer, his wit admire,
No one to help fulfil desire.
So while he slept, his spirit warm,
The Lord did conjure from his form
A maiden of such pulchritude,
She gave no hint of pending feud.

At dawn, when Adam gazed on Eve,
His heart rejoiced she'd never leave,
He harkened to her every word,
To ignore her just seemed absurd,

But then the Serpent bent her ear,
The Tree of Knowledge had no peer,
Eve took and bit the luscious flesh,
Gave some to Adam, so they'd mesh
With bonds they could appreciate.
The glory faded. All too late,
They stared bereft, the vision gone
And work alone would see it won
O'er many a millennial span.
Thus many a skirmish then began
And many days with struggles fraught
Did end in bitterness of thought.

Well, he blamed her and she blamed him
For standing by, his purpose dim,
Their only hope, the marriage bed,
And space. He built a garden shed!

Unpoetic

I've had enough of Keats and Pope,
Of Wordsworth, Blake and Wendy Cope,
I've had enough of *Sturm und Drang*,
Give me some Cockney rhyming slang!

The Nose That Interposes

The nose that interposes
Between your plate and you
Is a nose that never dozes
Till suppertime is through,
A nose that's always curious
When scenting tasty treats,
A nose that's quite censorious
If they're eaten out of reach.

The nose that sniffs the roses
By the summerhouse at dawn
Is a nose whose paws will process
The soil before it's done,
A bit of exhumation
Aerates a flowerbed
And hoarded bones are waiting
To be rescued from the dead.

The nose that teases hoses
Sprinkling water on the lawn
Is a nose whose tail proposes
That this element is fun,
It's fine in ponds and rivers
And fills a drinking bowl
But sudsy baths cause shivers
And merely make one howl.

The nose that tracks the postie
In luminescent gear
Is a nose whose bark's not ghostly
But suggests a force of ire,
It's game for space invaders,
Will recycle all the mail,
By habit, eco-friendly,
The bin's it's Holy Grail.

The nose that interposes
When the door is left ajar
Is a nose whose roving chooses
To corner cats beneath the car,
But then the dust will settle
And evening stills the paws,
The nose that's on its mettle
Sinks gently into snores.

Snow Limericks

Snow forecasts did not prescribe salt
causing traffic in winter to halt
and taxpayers' odium
at introuvable sodium
made teeth grit and find planning at fault.

Claimed drivers when ice capped their journey
Winter's stockpile of salt's not come early
This lack of base condiment
is a pain in the fundament
and calls for a hard-nosed attorney!

Something and Nothing

If nought plus one is one
And nought times one is nought,
The answer seems quite logical,
It doesn't leave me fraught.

And one divided by itself's
Still one our teachers claim,
How come that when you multiply
The answer's just the same?

Celebrity Hardback

I'm not a scaly tortoise
Who hibernates on straw,
I like a bit more light than that
Else I resort to law.

I'm not a lobster, either
Though my innards get devoured
With a relish that's unseemly,
It shows that I'm no coward.

I'm not a shiny beetle,
A ladybird or chafer,
I have an exoskeleton,
It keeps one's contents safer.

I'm not a crab or mollusc,
An insect or arthropod,
In fact I'm not invertebrate,
I have a spine! That's odd!

I come quite neatly packaged,
Boast a bold and brash design,
I migrate from shelf to table,
Not content with showing spine.

I'm full of information
With amazing tales to tell,
Of jetlag, parties and wild sprees,
Of stage and screen as well.

I'm popular as chocolate,
My lifespan's a small wonder,
When fifteen minutes fame is up,
The next one steals my thunder!

Making Waves

Miss Dickinson, who spoke of drowning,
Should have consulted Robert Browning,
Youth's crystal vision turned to rue,
Age would have proved was merely dew!

Bacchus Laureate

Oh, I'd like to be Poet Laureate,
the best literary ballgame around,
to chronicle functions
and royal conjunctions
would suit me down to the ground.

To muse on the subtext of history
might prompt an account in free verse,
but the annals of time
would ring with my rhyme
and the picture would be none the worse.

I could mention the cartwheeling verger,
the Queen's Diamond Jubilee spree,
and this year's Olympics,
those famous gymnastics
Threadneedle Street ponders with glee.

Yes, I'd love to be Poet Laureate,
There's a void since the fair Calliope**
no longer beguiles
on these emerald isles
ghosts of Milton and Dryden and Pope.

Some claim that the honour's a bind,
an appointment archaic and stuffy,
They can't follow Tennyson

and dear old John Betjeman,
nor Masefield, nor Motion, nor Duffy.

The title's undoubtedly grand,
though poets are used to grim hovels,
and rich Malmsey wine
as payment's just fine,
It's better reward than for novels!

But Ms Ayres and Ms Cope weren't contenders
and the accolade missed Mr Browning,
I don't stand a chance
on this side of France,
Like Ms Smith, I'm not waving but drowning.

So I don't think I'll make Poet Laureate,
but I swear I'm not twisted and bitter,
If finely-wrought talents
don't weigh in the balance,
I can always write haiku on Twitter!

**claiming poet's licence!*

Equilibrium

Humour is the only test of gravity, and gravity of humour; for a subject which will not bear raillery is suspicious, and a jest which will not bear serious examination is false wit.
Aristotle

Now here's a quote from Aristotle
His wisdom has me by the throttle
When life is grim, the joke is wry
I'm not sure, should I laugh or cry?

When life is comic, there's a sense
In which the tragic has expense
This is our fate, our crowning wreath
To die of mirth or quip at death.

English Languish

for June Casagrande

My Dad was one of those you cite
Correcting syntax as of right
A 'great big meany' to the core
He put construction to the fore
The spirit of the piece was lost
And in the basket ended tossed
The budding author withered then
And never showed him work again

My heart was shattered by the flaws
A split infinitive could cause
A misplaced preposition, too,
Could wreck a scene of derring-do
I quaked at the subjunctive mood
And clauses giving too much food
For thought midst plots that wouldn't hatch
And parts of speech that did not match

The hanging phrase is widely banned
And sentences that start with And
And sentences that start with But
Will cause an academic Tut!
The strict corrections they propose
Have blighted my immortal prose

O woe is me! I am undone!
There is no licence to have fun!

The muse is gone, I wonder why
My verse can't fit the needle's eye?
And art is left to hang its lyre
On weeping willows and expire
But now I think I've said enough
And must not brook this kind of stuff
My future work they'll not be faulting
I think the pedants are revolting!

One (Tax-Effective) Lump Sum, Or Two, Vicar?

"Zeal for your house consumes me." Psalm 69:9

We're looking on the bright side
That's where we cast our net
It's what the vicar tells us
Will get him out of debt
The choir's in perfect harmony
The organ chords resound
But if coffers are not *rustling*
There's no joy to be found

We've given in our widow's mite
But still it's not enough
Donations should be paper
Any other kind is duff
So forget about the small change
Dig deep in purse and pocket
If the tax-man doesn't take it
The vicar's sure to dock it!

Now those who've sung at weddings
Will know the cleric's drill
A captive congregation
Means collection plates should fill
He tells of crumbling plaster
And windows that need masons

Without a calm restraining hand
He'd be passing round large basins!

Some think an entrance turnstile
Would be a good idea
The takings would flow freely
And add up year by year
Such measures smack of mammon
And leave the punter skint
With work like that in progress
We should just install a Mint!

So render unto Osborne
The sums that must be found
And pray our Talents work for good
Unburied in the ground
With Faith and Hope and Charity
Investment's sure to double
But those who gather into banks
Heap up a hoard of trouble

You can't fault the Rev's intentions
His heart's for God and Church
Without his glorious vision
We'd all be in the lurch
He's anchor-man and mainstay
And shepherd of the flock
He keeps a strength of purpose
To make sure we build on rock

So we're looking on the bright side
We're hauling in our catch
The nets are fairly breaking
And debt we can despatch
Those future generations
Who want their sins forgiven
Can join with us who bless him
And have their Hope in Heaven!

Compass

So East is East
And West is West
And ne'er the twain shall meet
But heaven and earth
Are wedded spheres
God's Kingdom's in your street.